LIVING UNDER AIR ALERTS

From Home to Home

A calm, practical guide for families, schools and communities

Midas M&C Ltd.
and
Seamus O'Connor

LEGAL NOTICE AND DISCLAIMER

This publication is provided strictly for educational and informational purposes only. It does not constitute legal advice, medical advice, emergency response instruction, engineering guidance, or official civil defense direction. It does not replace instructions issued by local authorities, emergency services, or government agencies. While reasonable care has been taken to ensure clarity and accuracy, no guidance can eliminate all risk. Situations vary by location, building design, and circumstance. Neither Midas M&C Ltd., nor any affiliated or associated entities, employees, contractors, or representatives accept responsibility or liability for actions taken based on this publication. This material does not provide tactical, military, or operational instruction and is not intended for use in combat, security operations, or conflict planning.

- This publication does not replace formal training in emergency response or first aid.

Publisher and Attribution Author of Record: Midas M&C Ltd.

This publication is branded and distributed in cooperation with a Ukraine-based operating company, "з дому до дому." Front-cover branding and website reference reflect local outreach only.
www.3ddd.world

~ HOW TO USE THIS GUIDE ~

THIS GUIDE IS DESIGNED TO BE READ ONCE WHEN CALM AND REFERENCED WHEN NEEDED. YOU DO NOT NEED TO MEMORISE ANYTHING. YOU DO NOT NEED SPECIAL EQUIPMENT. YOU DO NOT NEED TO ACT HEROICALLY. THE PURPOSE OF THIS GUIDE IS SIMPLE: REDUCE FEAR BY INCREASING UNDERSTANDING. IT CAN BE READ INDIVIDUALLY, AS A FAMILY, OR IN CLASSROOMS AND COMMUNITY SETTINGS. CHILDREN DO NOT NEED TO UNDERSTAND EVERY DETAIL. CALM PRACTICES REPEATED OVER TIME IS ENOUGH.

YOU DO NOT NEED TO BE BRAVE,
YOU JUST NEED TO KNOW WHAT TO DO.

~ AUTHOR'S NOTE ~

THIS GUIDE WAS DEVELOPED BY MIDAS M&C LTD. FOR ONLINE EDUCATIONAL PURPOSES, IN CONJUNCTION WITH THE DIRECTOR, SEAMUS O'CONNOR, OF THE UKRAINE-BASED INITIATIVE З ДОМУ ДО ДОМУ.

MIDAS M&C LTD. IS A CONSULTING FIRM WITH A NICHE IN HELPING INDIVIDUALS AND COMPANIES WHO ARE OPERATING AT THE INTERSECTION OF RISK ANALYSIS, OPERATIONAL PLANNING, AND PUBLIC FACING COMMUNICATION IN COMPLEX ENVIRONMENTS; SHARE INVALUBLE KNOWLEDGE AND EXPERTISE. THE MATERIAL DRAWS ON STRUCTURED PROFESSIONAL EXPERIENCE SUPPORTING DECISION-MAKERS, ORGANISATIONS, AND CIVILIAN COMMUNITIES WHEN OPERATING UNDER CONDITIONS OF UNCERTAINTY, INFRASTRUCTURE STRESS, AND ELEVATED CONSEQUENCES.

THE PURPOSE OF THIS GUIDE IS NOT TO DESCRIBE EVENTS, ASSIGN RESPONSIBILITY, OR ANALYSE ANY OF THE CONFLICT DYNAMICS. ITS SOLE INTENT IS TO TRANSLATE ESTABLISHED PRINCIPLES FOR SAFETY, HUMAN BEHAVIOUR UNDER STRESS, AND UNMANGBLE RISK INTO CLEAR, CALM, AND ACCESSIBLE GUIDANCE FOR FAMILIES AND SCHOOLS.

EVERY EFFORT HAS BEEN MADE TO PRESENT INFORMATION RESPONSIBLY, CONSERVATIVELY, AND WITHOUT SENSATIONALISM. WHERE TECHNICAL CONCEPTS ARE REFERENCED, THEY ARE INCLUDED ONLY TO SUPPORT UNDERSTANDING AND REDUCE FEAR — NOT TO ENCOURAGE ANALYSIS OR SPECULATION.

THIS PUBLICATION REFLECTS AN INSTITUTIONAL COMMITMENT TO CLARITY, RESTRAINT, AND CARE, PARTICULARLY WHERE CHILDREN AND FAMILIES ARE CONCERNED.

TABLE OF CONTENTS

1.FEAR AND STRESS — WHAT IS HAPPENING INSIDE YOUR BODY

When an air alarm sounds, the body reacts before the mind has time to think. This reaction is automatic. It prepares the body to survive sudden danger. Adults and children may experience fear, shaking, rapid breathing, confusion, or a freezing feeling.

These reactions are all normal. They are not signs of weakness or panic. Loud alarms and unexpected sounds activate the nervous system before logic or reasoning can engage. A simple breathing reset can help reduce intensity:

1. INHALE SLOWLY THROUGH THE NOSE FOR 4 SECONDS.
2. HOLD GENTLY FOR 2 SECONDS.
3. EXHALE SLOWLY THROUGH THE MOUTH FOR 6 SECONDS.
4. REPEAT THREE TIMES.

A longer exhale signals safety to the nervous system. Children often experience fear without understanding why. They watch adults closely. Tone of voice, speed of movement, and facial expression matter more than explanations. Short, repeated phrases help:

- "SAFE PLACE NOW."
- "I AM WITH YOU."

As experiences are repeated, the brain begins to recognise familiar signals rather than treating each moment as entirely new. This recognition does not remove danger, but it reduces unnecessary alarm and allows calmer decisions to take place.

FEAR IS JUST THE BODY TRYING TO PROTECT YOU.

2. WHAT AN AIR ALARM MEANS

An air alarm means there may be a threat in the area. It does not mean an impact is certain. Modern missiles and drones are high-value military systems. They are most often used against specific military or critical infrastructure targets, guided by advanced systems designed to reduce errors.

This does not eliminate civilian risk. It does mean that danger is not random or constant. Your role as a civilian is not to be an analyst.

Your role is to follow a managble routine and focus on protection. To place yourself and your family in the best position possible until the threat level has reduced and we can return to our daily or nightly routines. While trying to responsibly manage our stress and maintain our own and our loved ones inner calm.

- Later in this book, you will see a list of the known air weapons that can be used and a breif summary.
- This is to bring further education and understanding, as shown to reduce trauma.

3. THE FAMILY PLAN — WHY ROUTINE MATTERS

Sometimes we have to plan for the unexpected.
A plan is not about knowing everything.
A plan is about knowing what happens next.
Routine reduces fear by removing uncertainty.

A SIMPLE ROUTINE:

1. ALARM SOUNDS.
2. AN ADULT SAYS: "SAFE PLACE NOW."
3. EVERYONE MOVES TOGETHER.
4. DOORS ARE CLOSED (NOT LOCKED).
5. EVERYONE SITS LOW, CLOSE TOGETHER.

ASSIGN ROLES IN ADVANCE.

- ONE ADULT GATHERS CHILDREN.
- ONE ADULT CHECKS LIGHTING OR DOORS.
- OLDER CHILDREN CAN HELP WITH SMALL TASKS.
- YOU DO NOT NEED TO ACT FAST.
- YOU NEED TO ACT THE SAME WAY EVERY TIME.
- CONSISTENCY INCREASES CALM.

4. WHY BUILDINGS AND BUNKERS PROTECT US

Buildings are not empty shells. They are designed to carry weight and remain standing. Some parts of buildings are stronger than others. Structural walls are thicker and designed to support the building. They provide better protection than thin interior walls.

Stairwells are usually among the most reinforced parts of apartment buildings. Once inside a stairwell:

- STAY AWAY FROM DOORS AND WINDOWS.
- STAY LOW, WORK ON BREATHING SLOW.
- REMAIN STILL AND CALM AS POSSIBLE.

1. Windows are weak points. Many civilian injuries result from broken glass rather than the initial explosions. Distance from windows matters more than room size.

2. Remember, You are placing strong structure between you and danger.

3. Bunkers often rank significantly higher for blast protection. being below the blast wave, removal of window and projectile threats. the primary evaluation for bunkers is based on ventalation, duration of stay, water, food communication to the outside world.

4. The most critical decision to make is how far is the distance to the bunker, how long are you exposed during relocation or transport to the bunker, is there any risk of gasses or water/flood situatons that could render the underground strucure unsafe.

NOTHING IS PERFECT AND OUR RISK MITIGATION STRATAGY MUST REFLECT THE MOST IMMEDIATE DANGER.

5. SOUND, TIME, AND DISTANCE

Light travels faster than sound. This is why you may see a flash before hearing a noise. A longer delay between light and sound usually means greater distance. Loud does not always mean close.

A simple grounding exercise is to count slowly and calmly after a flash is seen. The speed of sound is approximately 342 meters per second. * *As a general guide*: If more than 3 seconds pass between the flash and the sound, the strike was at least 1 kilometer away. To understand distance without the flash, we often look to measure time between the shockwave feeling and the sound. Shockwaves travel at a supersonic speed and can exceed 370 meters per second. This is the feeling that sinks our stomach and invokes fear immediately. However, if the sound and feeling are not simultaneous, there is likley a significant distance between us and the impact. Now, we can breath.

This does not remove all risk. It helps separate fear from immediate danger. Each time this is practiced, the mind moves from reflex toward recognition, allowing steadier responses. Multiple sounds may occur due to echoes and reflections. This does not mean danger is increasing.

HELPFUL PHRASES FOR CHILDREN:

- "THE BUILDING IS DOING ITS JOB."
- "SOUND TRAVELS FAR."
- "WE ARE SAFE HERE".

6. WHEN YOU CANNOT REACH A SHELTER

Not all families can reach shelters in time due to many reasons such as:

- POWER OUTAGES
- DISABLED ELEVATORS
- HIGH FLOORS
- MOBILITY LIMITATIONS

Rushing can increase risk. Correct use of structure where you are may be safer.

BEST OPTIONS:

- INTERIOR STAIRWELL
- INTERIOR HALLWAY AGAINST A THICK CONCRETE WALL
- BATHROOM WITH SOLID WALLS AND NO WINDOWS
- INTERIOR CORNER FORMED BY STRONG WALLS

1. Stay low. Stillness reduces injury risk.
2. If possible, try and place yourself in a place with at least 2 solid concrete walls between you and the exterior threat. If possible, consider the direction of the threat.
3. Position yourself accordingly.
   a. Away from the threat.
   b. Near an clear path to an exit stairwell.
   c. No loose objects on the ground.
   d. No windows.

* BETTER SAFETY STILL MAKES A DIFFERENCE.*

7. AFTER IMPACT
STAYING SAFE UNTIL HELP ARRIVES

Pause before moving and Ask ourselves and our peers or partners:

- IS THERE FIRE OR SMOKE?
- IS THE STRUCTURE DAMAGED?
- IS ANYONE INJURED?

If all answers are NO, remaining in place may be safer.

A GROUNDING EXERCISE FOR THE MINUTES AFTER AN INCIDENT:

USE THE 5–4–3–2–1 METHOD:

- **5 THINGS YOU CAN SEE**
- **4 THINGS YOU CAN FEEL**
- **3 THINGS YOU CAN HEAR**
- **2 THINGS YOU CAN SMELL**
- **1 THING YOU CAN TASTE OR ARE GRATEFUL FOR**

This gives the mind a familiar task and reduces shock.

Watch for secondary hazards:

- GAS SMELLS OR HISSING SOUNDS
- FLOODING OR STANDING WATER
- EXPOSED ELECTRICAL WIRING

Always try to Avoid open flames and standing water. Fire spreads quickly and after strikes, water can become electrically charged by damaged electrical systems.

Use flashlights or glow sticks so emergency workers can locate you and provide medical aid if needed. Stillness and visibility help others help you. Use your voice as neccessary, loud but clear, calm and in control.

8. PREPARING YOUR HOME

PREPARATION REDUCES FEAR.

NEAR YOUR SAFE PLACE, OR NEAR YOUR HOMES EXIT, KEEP:

- PHONE, CHARGER, BATTERY PACK
- DRINKING WATER
- ESSENTIAL MEDICATIONS
- FLASHLIGHT OR GLOW STICK
- STURDY SHOES
- COMFORT ITEM FOR CHILDREN, WARM CLOTHING.

<u>KEY TIPS</u>

- SECURE HEAVY FURNITURE. KEEP HALLWAYS CLEAR.
- PRACTICE THE ROUTNE CALMLY ONCE OR TWICE.
- MAKE COMPLETE COPIES OF ALL ESSENTIAL PERSONAL AND PROPERTY DOCUMENTS. HAVE THEM IN THE EMERENCY KIT WITHIN A SECURE FOLDER.

9. LIVING WITH REPEATED ALARMS

Repeated alarms can affect sleep, mood, and concentration. These reactions are normal. Routine, rest, and limiting exposure to distressing media support recovery.

DELAYED REACTIONS MAY APPEAR 24–72 HOURS LATER.

AFTER THE ALL CLEAR

When the all-clear signal is given, the body does not immediately return to normal. Adrenaline may remain elevated, causing tiredness, irritability, emotional flatness, or restlessness. At this stage, the brain is learning.

Each time a familiar sequence is recognised — alarm, safe place, waiting, all clear — the nervous system becomes better at distinguishing danger from recovery. Over time, this recognition reduces reflex responses.

HELPFUL ACTIONS:

- DRINK WATER
- SIT OR WALK SLOWLY
- EAT SOMETHING SIMPLE
- RETURN TO FAMILIAR ROUTINES
- KEEP VOICES CALM

CHILDREN MAY ASK QUESTIONS AFTER THE DANGER HAS PASSED. ANSWER SIMPLY AND HONESTLY.

REASSURE THEM:
- "IT IS OVER FOR NOW."
- "WE ARE SAFE."
- "YOU DID WELL."

SLEEP MAY BE LIGHTER THE FIRST NIGHT. THIS IS NORMAL.
RESILIENCE IS NOT TOUGHNESS.

IT IS RECOVERY - SUPPORTED BY UNDERSTANDING.

10. FAMILY QUICK REFERENCE

DURING AN ALARM:

- MOVE TO YOUR SAFE PLACE
- STAY LOW AND AWAY FROM WINDOWS
- USE CALM, FAMILIAR WORDS
- KEEP LIGHT AVAILABLE
- STAY TOGETHER

REMEMBER THESE KEY POINTS

1. Structure protects, Distance minimzes injuries.
2. Calm adults create calm children.
3. Light helps rescuers find you.
4. chaos breed chaos, hysteria creates panic.
5. when we panic, our cognitive thoughts, fine motor skills and processing information rapidly depretciate under stress. its normal to be sharper and critical under an emergency emotional state.
6. its our responsability to mange our own emotions and help others regulate thiers with patience.
7. we often face impossible decisions under these situations but arguing and unneccessary deliberationation only takes away valuable time.
8. decisions are often made on a basis of assumptions we make from our own tolerance of risk and fear. the responsible choice is always put saftey first for yourself and family.
9. its not about being '*right*' or '*strong*' its about making sure the family unit remains alive and with the least amount of danger or risk.
10. Set out your roles and tasks before hand, who does what. check eachothers steps and tasks briefly before heading to the safe place or shelter.

11. UNDERSTANDING PATTERNS, NOT PREDICTIONS (HOW THE BRAIN REDUCES FEAR THROUGH RECOGNITION)

We are going to make a slight shift in tone and direction to dive deeper into these topics; to include a more comprehensive and analytical assessment into the psychology and physics from a quantitative perspective. Pulling on the depth of experience and knowledge from Mr. O'Connor and his Wife, Tetiana. Whom has formal education and Master Degrees in Practical Psychology and Social Pedagogy, compounded with the personal experience, living in Ukraine throughout the entire conflict, after February 24, 2022. Furthermore, she has worked with a local university and taught hundreds of students learning english.

Tetiana's personal statement:

"The war in Ukraine coincided with my personal difficulties, such as returning to Ukraine from abroad, losing my father due to Covid. And then another emotional surge – the war in Ukraine. At first, there was hope that it would all end soon... Sleepless nights combined with the need to work made this time difficult from the beginning. At first there was fatigue, tension, exhaustion. Then, gradually, fear also appeared. Fear of repeated alarms, shelling, noise, sounds of air defense, shaheeds. Countless sleepless nights that exhausted the body and mind. And I still continue.

The human psyche is transformed in such times, acquiring features inherent in the environment. It becomes more unstable, pessimistic, anxious, expecting negativity. I can't say that this becomes a personal quality, but it definitely affects behavior, mood, and everyday life. Living in conditions where you constantly have to survive, push yourself to be happy, productive, socially active, and also physically healthy is a difficult test. I personally know many people who have acquired physical illnesses due to high and, apparently, consistently high cortisol. War affects both the psyche and the body.

The specificity of my work involves interaction with a large number of people, namely children and adolescents. I can conclude that children who are in Ukraine, they have inherent traits of restraint (it feels like a desire to protect themselves from the outside world), children are more sensitive, prone to tears, fear and panic during the educational process. That is, the war has an impact. I really hope that this period will pass and will remain only as an experience, without changing our personalities."

11.1 UNDERSTANDING PATTERNS, NOT PREDICTIONS (CONTINUED)

We can see, even with the most professional background and experience, our lived moments become our perceived reality. When fear becomes part of our reality, our judgment and sense of hope begins to feel clouded. To explain why familiarity, routine, and understanding reduce panic — grounded in neuroscience and psychology. We will start with how the brain reacts more strongly to uncertainty than to known risks.Pattern recognition shifts responses from reflex to regulation.

REPEAT EXPOSURE + EXPLANATION = REDUCED STRESS

This is how professionals manage high stress environments. Human beings respond to unfamiliar threats more intensely than to understood ones. When an event is unpredictable, the brain treats it as novel every time, triggering a full stress response. When patterns are recognized — the sound of an alarm, movement to a safe place, waiting, and the all-clear — the brain begins to categorize the event as known, even if it remains serious. We build a new '*normal*'.

This process does not remove danger. It reduces the severity of our internal alarm. Research in stress psychology and trauma recovery consistently shows that predictable routines and clear mental frameworks reduce panic responses and long-term anxiety symptoms, especially in children.

This is why calm repetition, simple explanations, and familiar actions are more protective than detailed warnings or emotional reassurance. Understanding the reality with facts and information become our biggest security blanket for our minds and in turn, our bodies.

Controlling the factors within our control helps reinforce stability and a feeling of management over an uncontrollable situation.

LeDoux, J. (2015). Anxious: Using the Brain to Understand and Treat Fear
National Institute of Mental Health – Stress Response Mechanisms
WHO – Psychological First Aid Guidelines

12. CIVILIAN RISK IS REAL — BUT NOT RANDOM

As living beings we often reduce catastrophic thinking by anchoring fear to actual distributions of risk.

In environments affected by air alerts, civilian harm is not evenly distributed across time or space. Multiple independent studies examining urban conflict environments show that the majority of strikes are directed toward specific military, industrial, or infrastructure targets rather than residential areas. This does not eliminate civilian risk. It means risk is uneven, not constant.

Large population studies from Ukraine, Israel, and other conflict-affected regions consistently show that civilian injury risk increases primarily due to proximity to:

- Strategic infrastructure
- Transportation nodes
- Military-related facilities

Understanding that risk follows patterns — rather than being random — helps the brain move from catastrophic thinking to situational awareness.

1. UN casualty mapping shows civilian harm clusters, not uniform spread
2. Residential injury risk drops significantly with distance from infrastructure
    a. **We understand in all conflict zones, there is the horrific realty outside of the statistics, that we all fear. However, in our planning, we must rely on what the statistical probabilities tell us and plan accordingly for the unforeseen events.**

UN Office for the Coordination of Humanitarian Affairs (OCHA), Civilian Harm Reports
UNAMA / OHCHR civilian casualty methodology papers
ACLED Conflict Event Data Project

13. THE PHYSICS OF DISTANCE, SOUND, AND PERCEIVED THREAT

When we ground our fear in the physical reality, without technical overload, we begin to add understanding; even to some of the most confusion situations.

Key concepts to remember:
Speed of sound vs light
Why loud ≠ close
Why echoes multiply sound perception in cities

Sound travels much more slowly than light. This is why flashes may be seen before sound is heard. In urban environments, sound reflects off buildings, creating echoes and overlapping noise. This can make distant events feel immediate. The human nervous system reacts to loudness, not distance. Understanding this distinction helps separate emotional reaction from physical proximity.

The simple practice of counting seconds after a flash is not about calculation. It is a grounding technique that places the mind back into time and space. Even rough estimates are sufficient to help regulate fear and support clearer thinking. Its in our control to back up our mental-health framing with evidence. Using reliable open source information and expanding our knowledge opens our horizons and allows us to handle all of life's situations better.

Longitudinal studies of populations living under repeated alert systems show that psychological outcomes are strongly influenced by predictability and perceived control. People with clear routine, consistent guidance, trusted information sources show lower long-term anxiety indicators than populations exposed to the same objective threat without structure.
For children in particular, repeated exposure paired with calm explanation reduces the likelihood of persistent fear responses.

THE GOAL IS NOT TO BECOME DESENSITIZED BUT TO GAIN SELF REGULATION.

14. CHILDREN, ADULTS, AND STRESS TRANSMISSION

To explain why adult calm matters more than explanations we have to understand things from what the children percive. Children do not assess danger independently. They assess the emotional state of adults. They regulate themsleves based on their immediate enviroment and the state of the parents and care givers.

Research consistently shows that children regulate their stress responses by observing their caregivers behavior — tone of voice, speed of movement, facial expression. Clear, repetitive language and calm physical presence helps reduce stress more effectively than reassurance or distraction.

Statements such as "I am with you" and "We know what to do" provide orientation and safety without minimizing reality. After an incident, children may process fear later. This delayed response is normal and should be met with patience rather than correction. Leading by example is one of the most essential character traits we can show as parents.

On that note, I would like to refresh our memory and key points on our safe place location and why this becomes our first line of defence. **READER REMINDER: This information is provided to reduce uncertainty, not to encourage recognition or analysis during alerts.**

Citations:

Israeli civilian resilience longitudinal studies
APA trauma adaptation research
WHO Mental Health in Emergencies reports
US National Weather Service – Lightning & Sound Distance Education
Open University Physics Resources – Sound Propagation
FEMA Public Education Materials
WHO Emergency Risk Communication Principles
FEMA Community Preparedness Framework
UNICEF – Children and Stress in Emergencies
APA – Trauma and Child Development
WHO – Caregiver Behavior in Crisis Settings

WHY BUILDINGS AND STRUCTURE MATTER
-SAFE PLACE NOW-

Modern buildings are not empty shells. They are engineered systems designed to carry weight, resist movement, and remain standing under stress.
Engineers design buildings to manage both vertical loads (the weight of the building itself) and lateral loads (forces such as wind, vibration, or shock). These forces are transferred through specific structural elements rather than being evenly distributed throughout the building.

Stairwells, elevator shafts, and central structural cores are typically among the most reinforced parts of an apartment building. They are commonly built with thicker concrete, steel reinforcement, and continuous vertical alignment. These elements are designed to remain intact even if non-structural walls, ceilings, or windows fail.
This distinction matters for civilian safety.

Data from engineering assessments and emergency response studies consistently shows that most civilian injuries in urban strike environments are not caused by direct impact, but by secondary risks and effects such as:

- shattered glass
- falling debris
- pressure changes
- uncontrolled movement during stress

Positioning oneself away from windows and behind structural walls places physical mass and engineered resistance between the body and these secondary hazards. The structure absorbs, deflects, and disperses energy before it reaches the people inside.

WHY BUILDINGS AND STRUCTURE MATTER...
-SAFE PLACE NOW-

No building can guarantee safety in all circumstances. However, engineering and disaster-response research shows that even modest increases in structural shielding significantly reduce the likelihood of injury. Being separated from a hazard by reinforced walls, interior corridors, or stairwells meaningfully lowers risk compared to open spaces or window-facing rooms.

This is why emergency guidance across different countries — despite differences in threat type, geography, or building style — converges on similar advice:

- **MOVE INWARD**
- **STAY LOW**
- **AVOID WINDOWS**
- **PLACE STRUCTURE BETWEEN YOU AND THE OUTSIDE**

These recommendations are not based on fear. They are based on how buildings work. Choosing a stairwell, central corridor, or reinforced interior wall does not eliminate danger. It reduces exposure — and in risk management, reduced exposure saves lives.

This guide is designed to support understanding and reinforce calm behavior patterns. It does not replace official instructions from authorities or Emergency Services.

No publication can account for all variables — building design, location, timing, or individual health conditions. The value of this guide lies in reducing fear-driven reactions and supporting safer decision-making under uncertainty. Used responsibly, it supports resilience without encouraging risk-taking or allowing a false sense of security from placing in unsafe situations, because we didn't know in better advance. Its all our responsibilities to continue to learn, grow and educate ourselves to understand risks accordingly.

WHAT IS THAT SOUND IN THE SKY?

Understanding does not increase danger — uncertainty does. For many civilians, air alerts are frightening not only because of the threat itself, but because the threat feels invisible and unknowable. When people cannot place events into a framework they understand, the mind fills the gap with worst-case assumptions. This appendix is included to reduce that effect.

The information that follows draws only on open, publicly available sources to explain — at a high level — the types of aerial systems that have been used against Ukraine. It is not intended to teach recognition, analysis, or response. Civilian guidance does not change based on weapon type.

Instead, this information helps place air alerts into context. It explains why alerts may last longer, why sounds can vary, and why the same protective actions remain effective regardless of the system involved. By replacing uncertainty with basic understanding, fear is reduced, decision-making improves, and families are better able to remain calm and focused on what matters: seeking shelter, staying together, and waiting safely for the all-clear.

WHY THIS INFORMATION IS INCLUDED

Some people assume that knowing more about weapons increases fear. However, In practice, the opposite is often true.

Fear grows fastest when events feel random, invisible, or unknowable. When people understand that threats follow patterns — and that their own behavior remains the same regardless of system type — anxiety decreases.

This appendix provides high-level, publicly available information about the main categories of aerial systems used against Ukraine. It explains what these systems are in simple terms, what open sources report about them, and — most importantly — what civilians should take away from that information.

NO PART OF THIS SECTION EXPLAINS:

- **How these systems are used tactically**
- **How to avoid detection**
- **How to respond differently based on weapon type**

For civilians, the advice remains consistent:
Seek structural protection, stay away from windows, remain calm, and follow official instructions.

HOW TO READ THIS SECTION

Each system below is described using four simple elements:

- What is it? – in plain language
- What open sources report – payload, range, speed (*approx.*)
- Identifiable characteristics – high-level category only
- Why it matters for civilians – emotional and behavioral context

All figures are approximate, as we understand each system can evolve.

Different sources report different values depending on variant, configuration, and conditions. Exact numbers are not important for civilian safety. Understanding the patterns is our priorty

THE LIST (OPEN SOURCE)

1. ONE-WAY ATTACK DRONES / LOITERING MUNITIONS

- Shahed-136 family (often referred to in Russian use as "Geran-2") (warhead commonly reported ~30–50 kg; range estimates vary widely). Reportts of a Geran-3 with larger payload and turbo engine.
- Decoy drones reported in mixed waves (e.g., "Gerbera" style decoys) (used to saturate defenses; specs vary)

2. AIR-LAUNCHED CRUISE MISSILES

- Kh-101 / Kh-102 (air-launched cruise missile family)
- Kh-55 / Kh-555 family (legacy air-launched cruise missiles, variants)
- Kh-59 family (example: Kh-59MK export specs published by Russia's federal export portal; note variant differences)
- Kh-69 (reported as used in the war; often discussed as derivative of Kh-59MK2; public specs vary)
- Kh-22 / Kh-32 family (large air-launched missiles; public specs vary; used in strikes)
- Kh-31 family (incl. Kh-31P anti-radiation in strike packages)

3. SEA-LAUNCHED CRUISE / ANTI-SHIP MISSILES, MODIFIED FOR USED IN LAND-ATTACK ROLE.

- 3M-14 Kalibr (SS-N-30A) land-attack cruise missile
- P-800 Oniks / Bastion (SS-N-26) supersonic cruise missile (also ground-launched via Bastion)
- 3M22 Zircon / Tsirkon (SS-N-33) hypersonic cruise missile (reported use; warhead/range reported in open sources varies)

4. BALLISTIC / AEROBALLISTIC MISSILES

- 9K720 Iskander-M (SS-26) short-range ballistic missile system
- Iskander-K (cruise-missile variant using 9M728/9M729 on Iskander launcher; public details vary)
- Kh-47M2 Kinzhal (air-launched ballistic missile)

WHAT WE KNOW

1. One-Way Attack Drones (*Shahed-Type / "Geran's"*)

- What are they?

One-way attack drones are unmanned aircraft designed to fly long distances and strike a target once.

What open sources report:

- Typical reported payload: approximately 30–50 kg
- Reported cruising speed: approximately 180 km/h
- Reported range: over 1,000 km, with estimates varying widely

Identifiable characteristics (*high-level*):

- Propeller-driven
- Delta or triangular wing shape
- Often launched in large numbers
- Why this matters for civilians
- These systems are commonly used in waves.
- This often leads to longer air alerts, repeated alarms, and extended periods of uncertainty.

For families, the key takeaway is endurance, not urgency.
Your actions remain the same.
The alert may last longer — that does not mean danger is increasing.

2. Long-Range Cruise Missiles (*Kh-101, Kalibr*)

- What are they?

Cruise missiles are jet-powered weapons designed to travel long distances at relatively low altitude.

What open sources report:

- Typical reported payload: approximately 400–450 kg
- Reported range: 1,500–2,500 km
- Speed: subsonic (slower than ballistic missiles)
- Identifiable characteristics (high-level)
- Winged missile shape
- Jet propulsion
- Used in planned strike packages

WHAT WE KNOW

2. Long-Range Cruise Missiles (*Kh-101, Kalibr*) continued,

Why this matters for civilians:

Cruise missiles are part of pre-planned operations, not spontaneous events. This reinforces an important reality:

- Air alerts are a precautionary early warning system
- They do not mean impact is immediate.
- For civilians, this supports calm, consistent behaviour rather than chaos. This warning gives us time to prepare, not panic.

3. Ballistic and Aeroballistic Missiles (*Iskander, Kinzhal*)

- What are they?

Ballistic missiles travel on a high, fast trajectory before descending rapidly.

What open sources report

- Reported payload: approximately 480–700 kg
- Reported range: 400–2,000 km, depending on system
  Speed: very high, especially during descent

Identifiable characteristics (*high-level*)

- Rocket-powered
- Very fast travel time
- Shorter warning windows in some cases

Why this matters for civilians:

These systems reinforce one consistent rule, Do not wait to see or hear anything, before going to our safe place. When an alert sounds, movement to a safe place should begin immediately.

4. Large Air-Launched Missiles (*Kh-22 / Kh-32*)
- What are they?

Large missiles originally designed for naval targets, also used against land targets, with modern changes.

What open sources report:
- Reported payload: up to ~1,000 kg
- Reported speed: **Mach 3–4+
- Reported range: ~600 km

Identifiable characteristics (*high-level*)
- Physically large missile class
- High speed
- Heavy payload

Why this matters for civilians:

These systems explain why structural positioning matters. Stairwells, reinforced walls, and interior spaces significantly reduce injury risk from secondary effects such as debris and glass.

MIXED STRIKE PATTERNS AND WHAT CIVILIANS SHOULD REMEMBER

Modern aerial attacks often involve multiple system types at once.
This does not require different civilian responses.

Regardless of system type:
- Distance from windows matters
- Structural mass matters
- Stillness reduces injury
- Calm adults reduce fear in children

Understanding that different systems exist helps the brain move away from catastrophic thinking and toward recognition.

THE TOP 11 THREATS

1) **Shahed-136 / "Geran-2"** type one-way attack drone.
- Category: One-way attack UAV (*loitering munition*)
- Warhead/payload: commonly reported ~30–50 kg (*variants reported higher*)
- Speed: commonly reported cruising ~180–185 km/h
- Range: open estimates often ~1,000–2,500 km (*varies by payload/variant*)
- High-level identifying characteristics: propeller-driven, delta-wing "flying wing" style; used in large waves.

Civilian relevance: often means prolonged alerts and repeated waves rather than a single short event.

2) **Kh-101 / Kh-102** (*air-launched cruise missile family*)
- Category: Air-launched cruise missile
- Warhead/payload: ~450 kg (*Kh-101 conventional; Kh-102 nuclear noted in open sources*)
- Range: ~2,500–2,800 km *(some reports claim higher*)
- Speed: subsonic; CSIS notes cruise speed ~Mach 0.58 (*max ~0.78*)
- High-level identifying characteristics: long-range winged cruise missile (*jet-powered*)

Civilian relevance: used in large, multi-system strike packages; emphasizes why consistent shelter routines matter.

3) **3M-14 "Kalibr"** (*SS-N-30A*)
- Category: Sea-launched land-attack cruise missile
- Warhead/payload: CSIS lists ~450 kg warhead
- Range: CSIS estimates ~1,500–2,500 km
- Speed: generally subsonic cruise *(typical for land-attack cruise missiles; Kalibr family varies*)
- High-level identifying characteristics: winged, jet-powered cruise missile; launched from ships/submarines

Civilian relevance: reinforces the "**Alarms are NOT Random**" concept—these systems are typically used in planned strike waves..

4) **9K720 Iskander-M** (*SS-26*) ballistic missile

- Category: Short-range ballistic missile (*road-mobile*)
- Warhead/payload: ~480–700 kg payload range reported by CSIS
- Range: ~400–500 km
- Speed: ballistic (very fast; CSIS provides system context; detailed phase speeds vary)
- High-level identifying characteristics: ballistic missile (*rocket-propelled*) launched from mobile launcher

Civilian relevance: shorter warning windows are possible, reinforcing "move early, don't window-watch."

5) **Iskander-K** (9M728/9M729 on *Iskander launcher*)

- Category: Ground-launched cruise missile variant using Iskander launcher
- Warhead/payload: public reporting includes ~480 kg warhead for 9M728/R-500
- Range: public reporting around ~500 km (*for cited variant*)
- Speed: cruise missile (*subsonic; varies by variant/source*)
- High-level identifying characteristics: cruise-missile class launched from the Iskander family launcher system

Civilian relevance: another reason why "distance from windows" remains a constant rule regardless of weapon type.

6) **Kh-47M2 "Kinzhal"**

- Category: Air-launched ballistic missile
- Warhead/payload: CSIS reports ~480 kg payload
- Range: CSIS reports ~1,500–2,000 km
- Speed: CSIS reports may reach up to Mach 10 (*ballistic-class speed; varies by phase*)
- High-level identifying characteristics: ballistic-class missile launched from aircraft

Civilian relevance: reinforces the importance of having a pre-decided safe place, there is no time for debate or argue.

7) **Kh-22** (*and derivative Kh-32 family*)

- Category: Large air-launched missile (originally anti-ship) used against land targets
- Warhead/payload: open sources commonly cite very large warhead (~1,000 kg for Kh-22)
- Range: open sources cite ~600 km for common variants
- Speed: open sources cite up to ~Mach 4+
- High-level identifying characteristics: very large missile class (size/weight category significantly larger than typical cruise missiles)

Civilian relevance: explains why some impacts can produce heavy structural damage and why stairwell/structural-wall positioning matters.

8) **Kh-59** and it's variants

- Category: Air-to-surface guided missile family (*variants*)
- Warhead/payload: Russian export portal lists penetrating warhead ~320 kg for Kh-59MK
- Range: Russian export portal lists up to 285 km (*variant-specific*)
- Speed: export portal lists in-transit speed ~900–1,050 km/h (variant-specific)
- High-level identifying characteristics: air-launched guided missile (*smaller class than strategic cruise missiles*)

Civilian relevance: supports the book's messaging that strikes can be mixed and varied; routines stay the same.

9) **S-300 missiles** (*air defense system; missiles sometimes used in ground attack role per reporting*)

- Category: Surface-to-air missile system family
- Warhead: CSIS lists ~133 kg (5V55) or ~143 kg (48N6) HE fragmentation warheads
- Range: CSIS notes missile variant ranges up to ~150 km (*variant dependent*)
- High-level identifying characteristics: ground-based air-defense missile family (many variants)

10) **P-800 "Oniks"** (*and the broader "Bastion" system use*)
- Category: Supersonic cruise missile (anti-ship origin; used against land targets)
- Warhead/payload: CSIS reports ~200–250 kg warhead depending on variant
- Range: CSIS reports ~300 km (*trajectory dependent*)
- Speed: CSIS reports up to ~Mach 2.2
- High-level identifying characteristics: supersonic cruise missile class (ramjet-powered)

Civilian relevance: supports the book's emphasis on structure and distance-from-windows rules.

11) **Medium-Range and Intermediate-Range Ballistic Missiles**
- What they are?

Medium-range and intermediate-range ballistic missiles are long-range rocket systems designed to travel very high above the atmosphere before descending rapidly toward a target. They are part of the same ballistic missile category as shorter-range systems, but operate over greater distances.

What we know publicly;
- Range: approximately 500–3,000 km (*medium-range*), with intermediate-range systems extending beyond that range.
- Payload: typically hundreds of kilograms, depending on the missile type and configuration[2]
- Speed: extremely high during descent, often several times the speed of sound[3]

Exact figures vary widely by system and variant and are not relevant for civilian decision-making. However, we encourage everyone to continue their own research and expansion through quality cited resources.

Identifiable characteristics:
- Rocket-powered
- Very high altitude trajectory
- Very rapid descent phase
- Shorter warning and reaction time once launched

Why this matters for civilians

- For civilians, the presence of medium- or intermediate-range ballistic systems reinforces one consistent principle:

Civilian safety guidance does not change with missile range. Longer-range systems do not create different shelter requirements, and they do not require civilians to make different decisions. What they do affect is warning time variability. In some cases, alerts may provide limited time between notification and potential impact.

This is why:
Safe locations should be identified in advance movement should begin immediately when alerts are issued window-watching or confirmation-seeking increases risk. Understanding that some systems travel very quickly helps explain why alerts must be taken seriously even when little information is available.

KEY POINTS TO REMBER:

- These systems are designed for long-distance strike, not for targeting individual civilians.
- Their inclusion in this guide is not to increase concern, but to reinforce preparedness through routine.
- Calm, early movement to a structurally protected location remains the most effective civilian response.
- These large scale and long range systems are very difficult for air defence systems to intercept, compounded with less warning time. It's paramount that we acknolodge this risk and our location in realtion to potential key target possabilities.

Such as:

- Strategic infrastructure, Transportation nodes
- Electrical distributon sites, Gas storage facilities
- Military-related facilities

CIVILIAN GUIDANCE REMAINS THE SAME,REGARDLESS OF SYSTEM TYPE.

A Final Word

Living under air alerts changes the rhythm of life. It introduces uncertainty into ordinary moments — meals, sleep, school, conversations. Over time, that uncertainty can quietly erode a sense of safety if it is not met with understanding, routine, and care.

This guide was written to offer something simple and durable: clarity. Clarity does not remove risk, and it does not ask people to be fearless. It helps people remain grounded, present, and capable — especially when others depend on them. Throughout this book, one idea appears again and again: preparation reduces fear. Not because it guarantees safety, but because it replaces helplessness with agency. Knowing where to go, how to stay protected, and how to recover afterward, it allows our mind to settle and body to respond more calmly.

There is one form of preparation that deserves special emphasis: basic medical knowledge. In moments of crisis, the first help available is often the people already there. Simple skills — controlling bleeding, recognizing shock, knowing how to support an injured person until help arrives — save lives every day. They also reduce panic, because people know they can act if needed. Learning first aid is not a sign that something terrible is expected. It is an act of care — for family, neighbours, students, and colleagues.

If possible, consider seeking basic first aid or emergency response training through recognized, reputable providers. These organizations offer evidence-based, civilian-appropriate education designed for real-world situations:

- The International Red Cross and Red Crescent Movement.
- National Red Cross or Red Crescent societies in your country.
- Recognised emergency medical training organisations approved by local health authorities.
- School-based or community first aid programmes offered by municipalities or NGOs

These programmes are designed to be accessible, practical, and supportive. They do not require medical backgrounds or special equipment. They build confidence quietly, over time. Preparedness is not about expecting the worst. It is about being ready to act — calmly and competently — if needed.

If there is one message to carry forward, let it be this:

- You do not need to control the events to live well within them.
- You need an understanding, routine, and the willingness to prepare together.
- Together Everyone Achieves More.

Stay connected.
Stay informed through trusted sources.
Care for one another — before, during, and after the all-clear.
Be patient and kind to one another.

That is how resilience is built.

CITATIONS:

Army Recognition, Shahed Drone Payload Analysis
Controverity Reminder, Shahed-136 Specifications
Calibre Defence, Evolution of Shahed-Type Strikes
CSIS Missile Threat, Kh-101 / Kh-102
CSIS Missile Threat, Kalibr (SS-N-30A)
CSIS Missile Threat, cruise missile profiles
CSIS Missile Threat, Iskander-M
CSIS Missile Threat, Kinzhal
CSIS Missile Threat, ballistic missile overview
Wikipedia / CSIS aggregated reporting, Kh-22
Wikipedia, Kh-22 speed characteristics
Wikipedia, Kh-22 range
SEPARATE CITATIONS PAGE
Sources and References (Public, Open Source)
Center for Strategic and International Studies (CSIS) – Missile Threat
Army Recognition
Reuters
UN OCHA and OHCHR civilian harm reporting
World Health Organization (WHO)
UNICEF
Eurocode / FEMA structural safety publications
Center for Strategic and International Studies (CSIS) – Missile Threat: Ballistic Missile Ranges
Stockholm International Peace Research Institute (SIPRI) – Missile and Payload Classifications
Arms Control Association – Ballistic Missile Characteristics
U.S. Congressional Research Service – Ballistic Missile Overview Reports

www.ingramcontent.com/pod-product-compliance
Lightning Source LLC
Chambersburg PA
CBHW061357240926
51846CB00007B/1435
9789692093941